Sherlock Holmes

Tony Lee

BAKER STREET W1

Badger Publishing Limited
Oldmedow Road,
Hardwick Industrial Estate,
King's Lynn PE30 4JJ
Telephone: 01438 791037

www.badgerlearning.co.uk

2 4 6 8 10 9 7 5 3

Sherlock Holmes ISBN 978-1-78464-010-1

Text © Tony Lee 2014

Complete work © Badger Publishing Limited 2014

The right of Tony Lee to be identified as author of this work has been asserted by him in accordance with the Copyright, Designs and Patents Act 1988.

Publisher: Susan Ross

Senior Editor: Danny Pearson

Publishing Assistant: Claire Morgan

Designer: Fiona Grant

Series Consultant: Dee Reid

Photos: Cover Image: © Gary Lucken/Alamy
Page 4: © Nikreates/Alamy
Page 5: © Nikreates/Alamy
Page 10: ITV/REX
Page 12: © PARIS PIERCE/Alamy
Page 13: Moviestore Collection/REX
Page 15: ITV/REX
Page 16: ITV/REX
Page 17: © Amoret Tanner/Alamy
Page 20: © Everett Collection Historical/Alamy
Page 21: © PARIS PIERCE/Alamy
Page 22: © AF archive/Alamy
Page 23: ITV/REX
Page 24: © AF archive/Alamy
Page 25: © Photos 12/Alamy
Page 29: © LAW AND CRIMES by VISION/Alamy
Page 30: © Steve Vidler/Alamy

Attempts to contact all copyright holders have been made.
If any omitted would care to contact Badger Learning, we will be happy to make appropriate arrangements.

Sherlock Holmes

Contents

Vocabulary

blackmailer	investigate
character	persuaded
detective	programmes
government	spin-off

1. Who was Holmes?

Lots of people like to read crime stories.

Some of the most famous crime stories were written by Sir Arthur Conan Doyle. His most famous character is a detective called Sherlock Holmes.

In the stories, people ask
Sherlock Holmes to solve crimes.

He is such a clever
detective that he usually
solves the crime
before the police!

Sherlock Holmes lives at 221b
Baker Street, in London, with
his friend Doctor Watson and
landlady Mrs Hudson.

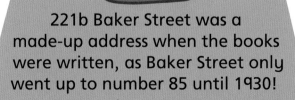

WOW! facts

221b Baker Street was a
made-up address when the books
were written, as Baker Street only
went up to number 85 until 1930!

2. Conan Doyle

Sir Arthur Conan Doyle wasn't always a writer. He was born in 1859 and trained to be a doctor.

At first, he did not have many patients so he started writing stories in his free time.

Then he found he liked writing stories more than being a doctor!

WOW! facts

Conan Doyle was a keen sportsman and he played golf, football and cricket. He even made ten first class appearances for Marylebone Cricket Club.

The first Sherlock Holmes story Conan Doyle wrote didn't sell very well and he nearly gave up writing detective stories.

But he carried on and, by the time he died, he had written four Sherlock Holmes books and 56 Sherlock Holmes short stories – and he was the most popular author of his time.

Famous stories by Conan Doyle

The Man with the Twisted Lip
1891

THE SIGN OF FOUR
1890

The Five Orange Pips
1891

The Adventure of the Speckled Band
1892

The Hound of the Baskervilles
1901

3. Sherlock's enemies

In the Sherlock Holmes stories, Holmes has to face some terrible criminals.

Some of his most famous enemies are:

Irene Adler

She is an actress, thief and blackmailer. She is one of the few people to ever beat Holmes, and many believe that he falls in love with her because of this.

Professor Moriarty

Moriarty is the secret boss of all of London's criminals.

In a story called *The Final Problem*, Moriarty seems to have killed Holmes at a waterfall in Switzerland!

But people were so sad that there would be no more Sherlock Holmes stories that they persuaded Conan Doyle to bring him back!

WOW! facts

Both Moriarty and Irene Adler only appear in one story, but they have become almost as famous as Holmes!

The Hound of the Baskervilles

One of the most famous of the Sherlock Holmes stories is called *The Hound of the Baskervilles.*

Sherlock and his friend, Dr Watson, travel to Dartmoor in Devon to investigate stories of a giant beast that has been heard howling on the moors.

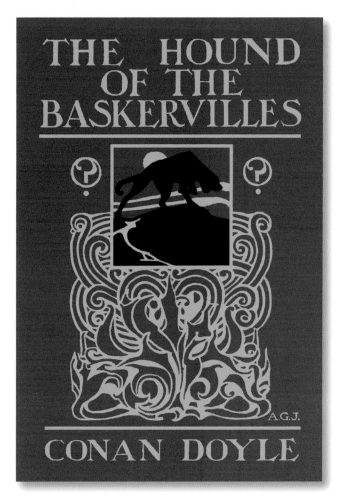

Sherlock Holmes finds out that the beast was just a huge dog. A criminal had trained the dog to kill off his relatives so that he could have all their money.

When Holmes faces the man on the moor, the man runs off in a panic but he gets stuck in a bog and drowns.

4. Allies and friends

Although the stories are about Holmes solving cases, he has help from lots of different people.

Mycroft Holmes

Mycroft is Sherlock Holmes' older brother. He is said to be even cleverer than Sherlock.

Mycroft works for the government and he often calls on his younger brother to help solve mysteries.

Doctor John Watson

Most of the stories are told by Dr Watson. He is Holmes' best friend.

Watson was a doctor in the army but he was injured in the Afghan War.

In the stories, Sherlock Holmes likes to show off. He often says that Watson misses important clues but Watson is still a big help to Holmes.

The Baker Street Irregulars

These are a gang of street kids that Holmes uses when he needs information from the street.

They only appear in three stories, but they have had many spin-off books, comics and TV shows based on them.

The police

The police often come to Sherlock Holmes to ask him to help them solve crimes.

Sherlock Holmes likes to show them how clever he is.

5. Journeys outside London

Most of Sherlock Holmes' cases start at 221b Baker Street but he often travels around the country to solve the mysteries.

Over the years, Holmes' 60 cases have taken him to...

London and the City	**31 times**
Surrey	**4 times**
Hampshire, East Sussex	**3 times**
Devon, West Sussex, Norfolk, Berkshire	**twice**
Herefordshire, Kent, West Midlands Cambridgeshire, Cornwall, Essex, South Yorkshire, Bedfordshire	**once**

As well as these places in the UK, Holmes has been to Switzerland – that was where he was nearly killed by Moriarty.

6. Holmes in the media

Over the years, more than 70 actors have played Sherlock Holmes on the stage, on radio, in films and on television.

These include:

William Gillette
He first played Holmes in 1899 on stage. In 30 years he played the detective over a thousand times!

CHARLES FROHMAN PRESENTS
William Gillette
IN HIS NEW FOUR ACT DRAMA
"SHERLOCK HOLMES"

SHERLOCK HOLMES

FAREWELL APPEARANCES *of* WILLIAM GILLETTE

1929-1932

WOW! facts

When William Gillette played the part of Sherlock Holmes he wore a deerstalker hat and smoked a pipe. Because of this, nearly every Holmes since has done the same!

Basil Rathbone

In the early 1940s, Rathbone played Holmes in 14 films.

Five of the films were not based on stories by Sir Arthur Conan Doyle.

In three of the films Holmes even fights the Nazis!

Jeremy Brett

Jeremy Brett played Sherlock Holmes on television in the 1980s and 90s.

There were 41 programmes and they were all based on stories by Sir Arthur Conan Doyle.

Lots of Sherlock Holmes fans think Jeremy Brett is the closest to how Sherlock Holmes would have looked.

Robert Downey Jr

In 2009 and 2011, Robert Downey Jr (who plays 'Iron Man') played Sherlock Holmes in two films.

The films were not based on stories by Arthur Conan Doyle.

Downey Jr played Sherlock Holmes as a slapstick character who was good at fighting.

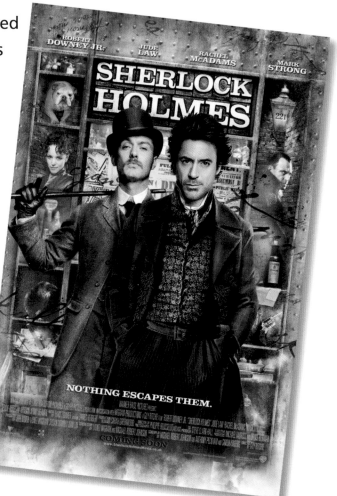

Benedict Cumberbatch

In 2010, the BBC made a new series about Sherlock Holmes called *Sherlock*. Benedict Cumberbatch played Sherlock Holmes.

The last three programmes were the most watched BBC drama series since 2001.

The stories were set in 21st Century London and were new stories but Sherlock still had to face his arch enemy, Moriarty.

7. Looking for clues

In every Sherlock Holmes story, Holmes uses the clues he can see to solve a case.

Here are some of the methods he uses:

Fingerprints

Holmes first mentions fingerprints as a way to identify a criminal in 1890, and he uses fingerprints to solve cases in many of his stories. The police didn't use fingerprints until over ten years after Holmes, in 1901!

Footprints

Almost half of the 60 stories have footprint evidence used.

It's not just the size of the foot that can identify a criminal, but also the mud, clay, dirt or even blood on the sole of the shoe that can solve a case.

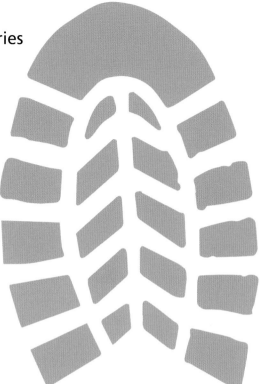

Observation

Holmes is famous for noticing things other people might not notice.

Holmes would see everything, every little detail on an item.

Think of your pencil.

What colour is it?

How long is it?

Does it need sharpening?

(If you needed to look, then you need to train yourself to be more observant!)

Listening

Often people thought Holmes was not really listening to what they said. But, in fact, he was listening to all sorts of things he could learn about the person.

He could tell where the person came from by the way they spoke and he could also tell if they were lying or not!

Questions

Name the author who thought up the character Sherlock Holmes. *(page 5)*

When was *The Hound of the Baskervilles* written? *(page 9)*

In which war was Dr Watson injured? *(page 15)*

How many times did Holmes travel to Surrey? *(page 18)*

Who played Sherlock in the 2009 film? *(page 24)*

What year did the police start to use fingerprints to help solve crimes? *(page 26)*

Index